Childhoods
of the
Presidents

George W. Bush

Childhoods *of the* Presidents

John Adams

George W. Bush

Bill Clinton

Ulysses S. Grant

Andrew Jackson

Thomas Jefferson

John F. Kennedy

Abraham Lincoln

James Madison

James Monroe

Ronald Reagan

Franklin D. Roosevelt

Theodore Roosevelt

Harry S. Truman

George Washington

Woodrow Wilson

George W. Bush

Bill and Dorcas Thompson

Mason Crest Publishers
Philadelphia

Produced by OTTN Publishing, Stockton, New Jersey

Mason Crest Publishers
370 Reed Road
Broomall, PA 19008
www.masoncrest.com

First printing

1 3 5 7 9 8 6 4 2

Library of Congress Cataloging-in-Publication Data

Thompson, William, 1931-
    George W. Bush / Bill and Dorcas Thompson.
        p.   cm.   (Childhood of the presidents)
    Summary: A biography of the forty-third president of the United
    States, focusing on his childhood and young adulthood.
    Includes bibliographical references (p.) and index.
        ISBN 1-59084-281-2
    1. Bush, George W. (George Walker), 1946-   —Childhood and
    youth—Juvenile literature. 2. Bush, George W. (George Walker),
    1946-   —Juvenile literature. 3. Presidents—United States—
    Biography—Juvenile literature. [1. Bush, George W. (George
    Walker), 1946-   —Childhood and youth. 2. Presidents.]
    I. Title. II. Series.
    E903.T48 2003
    973.931'092—dc21
    [B]   2002069221

Childhoods
of the
Presidents

Table of Contents

★★★★★★★★★★★★★★★★

Introduction...6
Arthur M. Schlesinger, jr.

A Surprise Attack!...............................9

Beginnings 13

The Midland and Houston Years 17

Becoming a Leader at Andover 29

From Texas to the White House 35

Chronology..42

Glossary...43

Further Reading...................................44

Internet Resources 45

Index...46

★ *Introduction* ★

Alexis de Tocqueville began his great work *Democracy in America* with a discourse on childhood. If we are to understand the prejudices, the habits and the passions that will rule a man's life, Tocqueville said, we must watch the baby in his mother's arms; we must see the first images that the world casts upon the mirror of his mind; we must hear the first words that awaken his sleeping powers of thought. "The entire man," he wrote, "is, so to speak, to be seen in the cradle of the child."

That is why these books on the childhoods of the American presidents are so much to the point. And, as our history shows, a great variety of childhoods can lead to the White House. The record confirms the ancient adage that every American boy, no matter how unpromising his beginnings, can aspire to the presidency. Soon, one hopes, the adage will be extended to include every American girl.

All our presidents thus far have been white males who, within the limits of their gender, reflect the diversity of American life. They were born in nineteen of our states; eight of the last thirteen presidents were born west of the Mississippi. Of all our presidents, Abraham Lincoln had the least promising childhood, yet he became our greatest president. Oddly enough, presidents who are children of privilege sometimes feel an obligation to reform society in order to give children of poverty a better break. And, with Lincoln the great exception, presidents who are children of poverty sometimes feel that there is no need to reform a society that has enabled them to rise from privation to the summit.

Does schooling make a difference? Harry S. Truman, the only twentieth-century president never to attend college, is generally accounted a near-great president. Actually nine— more than one fifth—of our presidents never went to college at all, including such luminaries as George Washington, Andrew Jackson and Grover Cleveland. But, Truman aside, all the non-college men held the highest office before the twentieth century, and, given the increasing complexity of life, a college education will unquestionably be a necessity in the twenty-first century.

Every reader of this book, girls included, has a right to aspire to the presidency. As you survey the childhoods of those who made it, try to figure out the qualities that brought them to the White House. I would suggest that among those qualities are ambition, determination, discipline, education— and luck.

—ARTHUR M. SCHLESINGER, JR.

President George W. Bush shakes hands with rescue workers near the ruined World Trade Center in New York City. The president won praise for his leadership after the terrorist attacks of September 11, 2001.

A Surprise Attack!

"**M**r. President! Mr. President! There's an unidentified aircraft heading toward the White House!" It was nearly midnight on September 11, 2001, and President George Walker Bush was beginning to drift off to sleep. His wife, Laura Bush, was already fast asleep beside him. As they heard the voice of the Secret Service agent, they jumped up, grabbed their dogs Barney and Spot, and took the elevator to rooms deep beneath the White House. This area, called the Presidential Emergency Operations Center, was a place where President Bush sometimes held meetings with members of his National Security Council.

Earlier that day, President Bush had been in Florida. While he was visiting a class of elementary-school students, an aide whispered into his ear. Terrorists had flown two airplanes into the World Trade Center in New York City and another into the *Pentagon* outside Washington, D.C. A fourth plane, possibly heading to the White House or the Capitol, had crashed in western Pennsylvania. Thousands of people had been killed and many others had been wounded in the attacks. As soon as he could, President Bush boarded *Air Force One*. By that

Rescue workers in New York City cheered President Bush when he visited the site of the World Trade Center after the terrorist attack.

evening he was back at the White House.

The unidentified aircraft that had disturbed the Bushes' sleep turned out to be a U.S. Air Force jet guarding the skies over Washington, D.C. These precautions showed the dramatic changes that were already taking place in the United States because of the attacks. President Bush would need to comfort the nation and prepare its people to respond to these terrorist attacks.

Before September 11, the country had been divided in its views on President Bush. In the months after the attacks, however, most Americans agreed the new president was doing a remarkable job handling the crisis. In late September, the *New York Times* wrote, "[George W. Bush] was becoming the kind of leader we need. And when he mourned victims and comforted survivors and rallied the nation from the rubble, he began to discover his best." By the end of the year, in a *Time* magazine recap, historian Michael Beschloss wrote, "A President must make sure that if he is getting the U.S. into a war, it is for a purpose that is worth it. Second, he must make sure that he tells the American people at the outset how costly this might be. In both cases I think Bush has done amazingly well."

At the White House, the Bushes have two dogs, Spot and Barney, and a cat named India.

Having produced two U.S. presidents and a governor of Florida (Jeb), the Bushes must be considered one of America's most prominent political families.

What experiences had prepared George Walker Bush for the task of being president? How was he equipped to lead a shocked and grieving nation in the aftermath of September 11? In order to understand him, we need to look back at his life, beginning with his parents.

The future 41st president plays with his baby son, the future 43rd president.

Beginnings

George W. Bush's family has been living in America for a long time. His father, George Herbert Walker Bush, was descended from the Bush family that sailed from England in the 1600s and settled on Cape Cod, Massachusetts. His mother, Barbara Pierce Bush, is a descendant of Franklin Pierce, the 14th president of the United States. The Pierce family's roots also date back to 17th-century America.

George's father and mother met and fell in love when they were in high school. Right after his graduation in 1942, however, George H. W. Bush enlisted in the U.S. Navy as a pilot. The United States had entered the Second World War at the end of 1941, after the Japanese attack on Pearl Harbor. On one mission in September 1944, George Bush's plane was shot down near an island held by the Japanese. After several hours in the water he was rescued by an American submarine.

After George returned from the war in 1945, he and Barbara were married. The young couple moved to New Haven, Connecticut. There, George attended Yale University and Barbara found out they were going to have a baby. "I was huge and weighed more than a Yale linebacker," she wrote in her memoirs. "Yes, I was pregnant with our first child."

George Walker Bush was born on July 6, 1946. "George and I were mad about our baby," Barbara wrote. They called him "Georgie."

After graduating from Yale in June of 1948, Georgie's father (now nicknamed "Poppy") accepted a job in Texas with Dresser Industries, an oil company. The 24-year-old drove to Odessa, Texas, to find a place for his family to live.

A week later, Poppy called Barbara to say he had found a "sorry little house." When Barbara and two-year-old Georgie arrived at their new home, they found West Texas far different from the green woods and rolling hills of Connecticut. It was flat, treeless, and barren. "Nothing comes easy to West Texas," Barbara later wrote. "Every tree must be cultivated and every flower is a joy."

Their first home in Odessa was a small apartment. They shared a bathroom with the neighbors in the next apartment (most people on their street had *outhouses*). They also had a refrigerator—the only one in the neighborhood.

Georgie was an active boy. Not long after the Bushes arrived in Odessa, Poppy wrote to a friend, "You should see Georgie now. . . . He is really cute, I feel. Whenever I come home, he greets me and talks a blue streak, sentences disjointed of course but enthusiasm and spirit boundless. He is a real blond and pot-bellied. He tries to say everything and the results are often hilarious. . . . He seems to be very happy wherever he is and he is very good about amusing himself in the small yard we have."

In the spring of 1949, Poppy Bush was transferred to

Young George with his parents, Barbara and George H. Bush, and his grandparents, Dorothy and Prescott Bush, at the airport in Odessa, Texas. Prescott Bush was a United States senator.

California to learn more about the oil business. He worked all over the state in other plants owned by Dresser Industries. Around this time Barbara became pregnant with their second child. In December of 1949, Georgie got a little sister, Pauline Robinson, nicknamed "Robin."

In 1950 Poppy Bush was transferred back to West Texas. This time the Bushes settled in Midland, a town 20 miles east of Odessa. It was in this city that Georgie, then four years old, began to develop his lifelong love of Texas and its people.

The Midland and Houston Years

*B*ack in 1880, the Texas Pacific Railroad began to lay track west from Fort Worth, Texas. At the same time, the Southern Pacific started laying track east from El Paso, Texas. Midland was settled where the tracks of these two railroad companies met. For years Midland was just another dusty West Texas town. In 1923 oil was found 80 miles to the south. Soon Midland prospered, becoming the home of millionaire oilmen as well as oil-company employees.

George W. Bush lived in West Texas until he was 13. He has said living in Midland helped make him the kind of adult he became. "I don't know what percentage of me is Midland, but I would say people, if they want to understand me, need to understand Midland and the attitude of Midland," he told the *New Yorker*. Young George learned to love the big Texas sky, the wide-open views, and the closeness of the people.

The Bush family lived in a small blue house in Midland. Their neighbors came from all over the country, and most

George W. Bush loved almost everything about his West Texas childhood. He especially liked the cowboy clothes.

Sunset near Midland. Oil shaped George's hometown as well as the fortunes of the Bush family.

were also newcomers to Midland. There were many young couples with children in the neighborhood, so Robin and Georgie had no shortage of friends to play with. Georgie was growing into what his dad called "a near-man," even though he was only four and a half. Georgie loved to wear Texas cowboy clothes and almost lived in them.

One of Poppy Bush's friends was John Overbey, who lived just across the street from the Bushes. George Bush and John Overbey talked often about forming their own company. In 1951, the two men started the Bush-Overbey Oil Development Company and opened offices in downtown Midland.

Georgie was busy making friends too. One was another four-year-old boy, Randy Roden, who lived next door. Georgie and Randy would sometimes go out to the oil fields with

Poppy Bush. They would ride in a station wagon past rows of oil derricks that pumped day and night. While listening to the clank of machinery, Georgie and Randy would settle down in the car and sleep while Mr. Bush checked the wells.

When Georgie was almost six, the family moved into a new home across town. This house had a large front yard, three bedrooms, and even some oak trees. Georgie kept in touch with his first friend, Randy, and often invited him over to spend the night. Yet Georgie made many other friends and played outdoors with them as much as he could.

Georgie loved to ride his bike all over town with his friends and run around nearby homes. Neighbors who watched him dart through yards and climb over fences called him "Bushtail." In the 1950s Midland was the kind of town where young people had many adults watching over them. Once Georgie ran out of a friend's house into the street without looking. His friend's mother ran out yelling at him. He never did it again!

At Sam Houston Elementary School, young Georgie showed the humor and playfulness that he would be known for all his life. Once, in the third grade, he was bored when the class had to stay inside because of rain. He decided to pass a football with a friend and threw it right through the window. When he was in the fourth grade, Georgie painted a mustache, goatee, and sideburns on his face with a ballpoint pen. His teacher sent him to the principal's office, where he received a stiff warning. It didn't seem to bother Georgie.

In February of 1953, a third Bush child, John Ellis Bush, was born. The family nicknamed him Jeb.

Just a month after Jeb's birth, Mrs. Bush noticed that something was wrong with three-year-old Robin. She acted tired and had developed bruises on her body. At the local hospital, tests showed that Robin had a disease called *leukemia.* George and Barbara took their daughter to New York City, where Mr. Bush's uncle was the president of Memorial Sloan-Kettering Hospital, a famous cancer research center.

For the next seven months, the Bushes traveled back and forth between New York and Midland. Georgie didn't know how serious Robin's condition was; he only knew that his sister was sick. When Robin did return to Midland from time to time, Georgie was told simply that he couldn't roughhouse with her the way he had before. She might *hemorrhage* if their play was too rough.

However, there was nothing the doctors could do for young Robin. In October 1953, she died in New York. The Bushes had the difficult task of telling their son about Robin's death.

The Bushes arrived in Midland while Georgie was at school. When he saw his parents' car, he ran to welcome his parents and his sister. He was sure he saw Robin's head through the car window. He was shocked when he was told that his sister was dead.

"Those minutes remain the starkest memory of my childhood," said George Bush over 40 years later, "a sharp pain in the midst of an otherwise happy blur."

It is difficult to know what permanent effect Robin's death may have had on George W. Bush. As an adult he has said that he learned not to take life for granted, but to live each day fully and enjoy it, no matter what happened. Some people

Robin Bush, George's younger sister. Her death from leukemia in 1953 was, he recalled years later, "a sharp pain in the midst of an otherwise happy blur" of childhood.

believe that his tendency to be funny and to try to lift people's spirits may be a result of his sister's death.

Elsie Walker, Georgie's cousin, has said, "I do think that the death of Robin had a big effect on George. I think it's very, very difficult for a young child to see his parents suffering. And so I think he tried to be lighthearted. . . . I think kids who lose a *sibling* often try and find ways to, you know, make things easier in the family."

After Robin died, it seemed that young George felt a responsibility to care for his mom, especially when his father was traveling. He wanted to help her with housework. But more than that, he wanted to cheer her up. Georgie tried to

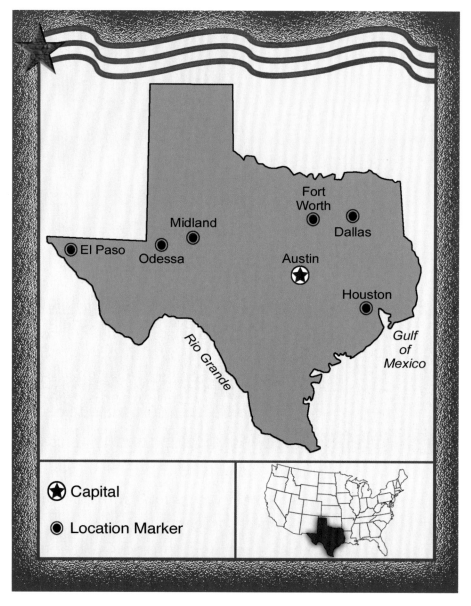

This map of Texas includes the towns where George W. Bush spent much of his childhood, Odessa and Midland.

entertain her—to make her laugh and not be sad.

At first, his mother wasn't aware of what her grieving was doing to her son. Then one day Barbara Bush overheard

Georgie talking to a friend of his. Georgie told the friend that he couldn't play right then because he had to stay with his mother, who needed him. Mrs. Bush realized that her sadness was too much of a burden for a seven-year-old. She needed to let him be a little boy again.

Georgie and his mother always had a special bond. With his father often away from home, she was the one who *nurtured* and disciplined him. His mother attended all of his Little League games and often kept score. Georgie developed Barbara Bush's quick wit. A family maid once said, "He was definitely like his mother, they were exactly alike, even their humor was alike."

At the same time, Georgie had a great admiration and respect for his father. Though Barbara was the one who handled small problems, Poppy Bush always took care of bigger offenses. "I would scream and carry on," Barbara Bush has said about their discipline styles. "The way George scolded was by silence or by saying, 'I'm disappointed in you.' And [the children] would almost faint."

The Bushes liked to spend time away from Texas with their children. Every other summer the Bush family went to Maine, where Georgie's great-grandparents, the Walkers, had a beautiful oceanfront home. There, at Walker's Point in Kennebunkport, Georgie's parents were able to relax. The Bush children also loved visiting the Maine coast, but Georgie still preferred the flat Texas countryside.

In Midland, where every

> Georgie had all kinds of nicknames in Midland. These included Googen, Junior, Bombastic Buskin, Little Bush, and Shrub.

George may have been more like his mother in personality—sharing, among other things, her quick wit—but he deeply admired his father.

boy seemed to belong to Little League, Georgie developed his lifelong love of baseball. Poppy Bush had been an excellent athlete. He frequently played ball with Georgie, who was a catcher. Georgie felt he had made it when his father told him one day that he no longer had to worry how hard he threw to his son. Georgie could handle whatever his father threw at him.

A few months before Georgie was 10, Poppy wrote his father-in-law, "Georgie aggravates . . . me at times (I am sure I do the same to him), but then at times I am so proud of him I could die. He is out for Little League—so eager. He tries so very hard. It makes me think back to all the times I tried out.

. . . He has good fast hands and even seems to be able to hit a little. I get as much kick out of watching him trying out as I do out of all our varied business efforts."

Georgie loved knowing facts about baseball and memorized the statistics of major-league players. He collected baseball cards and mailed them off to be autographed by his favorite players. His hero was Willie Mays, so Georgie read everything he could about the Giants' slugger.

While young George enjoyed his years in Midland, his father formed another company, Zapata Company, and began drilling for oil 70 miles east of Midland. The business was successful, and George H. W. Bush became a millionaire. In 1955 the Bush family moved again. This time the home was much larger and had a swimming pool.

In January of that year, the Bush children welcomed a new little brother into the family, Neil Mallon. In October 1956, George and Barbara had their fourth son, Marvin.

In 1958 Georgie entered the seventh grade at San Jacinto Junior High School. During that school year, he was elected president of his class. He was happy and popular. Georgie didn't know that the seventh grade would be his last school year in West Texas.

In 1959 Zapata split into two companies, and Poppy Bush became president of the Zapata-Offshore Company. He began to concentrate on drilling for oil in the Gulf of Mexico. Midland was too far

Young George loved to play any game and was very competitive. One of his friends later said that when Georgie started a game, he often wanted to keep playing until he won.

inland from this new business. In the summer of 1959, when Barbara was pregnant with their sixth child, the family moved to Houston, 500 miles away.

That change was hard for Georgie. He never forgot the security he had felt in West Texas. "Midland was a small town, with small-town values. We learned to respect our elders, to do what they said, and to be good neighbors. We went to church. Families spent time together," he has said. "It was a happy childhood. I was surrounded by love and friends and sports." All he had known since he could remember was hot, dusty, and dry Midland, where he felt at home with everyone. In Houston he found himself in the largest city in Texas, an area that was green and wet. Everything there felt damp to Georgie.

In August of 1959, just as the Bush family moved into a spacious new home, the last of the Bush children was born. A girl, they named her Dorothy Walker Bush and called her "Doro." The four boys gathered around to see their new baby sister and listened as their father remarked on how much she looked like them.

The wealthy neighborhood, the big city, the different climate, and the new sister were not the only changes for Georgie. He was enrolled in a private school for the first time in his life. He began eighth grade at Kinkaid, a college preparatory day school and one of the oldest in the state.

Georgie adjusted quickly to his new life. At Kinkaid, he became involved in many sports, especially baseball. He participated enthusiastically in debate and speech tournaments. He was well liked and popular and related easily to everyone

The Bush brothers with their father. From left: Neil, Poppy Bush, Jeb, George W., and Marvin.

he met. He was a class officer and an A student at Kinkaid.

While the Bush family lived in Midland, Poppy Bush had become involved in politics and the Republican Party. That interest increased in Houston. Young George fit right in and thoroughly enjoyed the political activities. At parties in the Bush home, or at fund-raisers, the eighth grader greeted all the guests when they arrived and made sure he said good-bye when they left.

During his ninth-grade year, his parents began to talk to him about sending him to Phillips Academy, an all-boys boarding school in far-off Andover, Massachusetts. Both his father and grandfather had attended this prominent private school. Before the end of his freshman year at Kinkaid, the Bush family learned that George had been accepted at Phillips. He left for the academy in the fall of 1961 to begin his sophomore year.

At Phillips Academy, George W. Bush discovered his leadership abilities when he became the school's head cheerleader.

Becoming a Leader at Andover

*P*hillips Academy, also known as Andover, sits on a 500-acre campus 20 miles outside Boston. Founded in 1778, it is as old as the United States. George's father and grandfather had been outstanding students there. His father had been named "Best All-Around Fellow" at his graduation in 1942 and was still remembered by some members of the faculty when young George arrived on campus 19 years later.

The shock of moving again, this time nearly 2,000 miles away from family and friends, must have been great. And when George arrived, he found the academy very different from what he was used to. He remembers, "Andover was cold and distant and difficult. In every way, it was a long way from home. . . . Forlorn is the best way to describe my sense of the place and my initial attitude."

He also had to adjust to the strictness and formality of Andover. The school was run by a West Point graduate who demanded that *demerits* be given to any student who was late for classes or assemblies. Chapel was mandatory five days a week. Students were required to wear a jacket and tie to chapel and to any appointments. This was quite a change from George's casual dress in Texas.

On top of this, George found his classwork more difficult than anything he had known before. He and some of the other students from Texas felt that academically they were behind students from the East Coast. He recalls writing his first essay for English class, about the death of Robin. When he wrote about crying after her death, he decided to look up a *synonym* for the word *tears* in his **thesaurus**. Hoping to impress his teacher, he changed *tears* to **lacerates**. Unfortunately, that word is a synonym not for the liquid that comes out of our eyes when we cry, but for the verb that is pronounced with a long "a" sound and that means to cut or rip apart. George received a bad grade on his paper. He wondered if he could make it at Andover.

George decided to work hard. He found support among the 18 other Andover students from Texas. They often studied together late into the night. He became a member of the Spanish Club and discovered a love for history that stayed with him. He fondly remembers his history teacher, Tom Lyons. "He taught me that history brings the past and its lessons to life," George wrote, "and those lessons can often help predict the future."

George played junior varsity baseball and football in his first year. However, he realized he couldn't compete with the best athletes at Andover and looked around for another school activity. He joined the eight-man cheerleading staff, whose job was to raise the spirit of the student body. Soon he became head cheerleader and planned skits used at school assemblies.

No one had ever done that job quite like George. One picture taken in those years shows him and the other cheerleaders wearing skirts. In another, you can see the whole staff crammed into a telephone booth.

The dean of students, Mr. Benedict, wanted George to tone down some of his skits. The school newspaper, however, defended the head cheerleader. Eventually George won the dean over. As a *New York Times* article related: "In the end, Mr. Benedict grew extremely fond of George. The next head cheerleader, Michael M. Wood, said he was taken aside by Mr. Benedict and told that George had raised Andover's school spirit to its highest level since Mr. Benedict had joined the school, in 1930."

George also organized an intramural stickball program—and it made him famous at the school. Stickball was played with broomsticks and a tennis ball on a field. It had been informally played at the school for years. However, George decided in his senior year to form a stickball league with different teams wearing their own special shirts. The season would end in a grand-championship game.

He announced this to the student body at a school assembly while wearing a top hat. He gave an *impromptu* 20-minute speech that had his fellow students laughing. "I was his roommate [at the time]," remembered John Kidde. "He announced how he was high commissioner of

Oliver Wendell Holmes, a U.S. Supreme Court justice, and Samuel Morse, who developed the telegraph, are just two of the many famous people who attended Phillips Academy before George W. Bush arrived.

stickball, and he got some chuckles, and he just kept going. He was making it up as he went along. And he started talking about rules, and it . . . was a riot."

Years later, many who were at the academy remember George W. Bush as a person who could get along with anyone. One of them, José R. Gonzalez, said, "A guy from Puerto Rico

An autumn scene from the campus of Phillips Academy. George W. Bush graduated from the prep school in 1964.

was sort of unusual at Andover, but it didn't bother [George]." José spent Thanksgiving with George at his grandfather's house in Connecticut. It was only during this visit that José realized George's grandfather, Prescott Bush, was a U.S. senator.

> George's dormitory at Andover was called America House because in 1832 the song "America" had been written there by Samuel Francis Smith.

George had the reputation at Andover of being a friendly guy who was always enjoying himself. "My memory of living with George was that it was probably the funniest year of my life," said another former roommate. "George is just an incredibly funny guy. He had a way of keeping everything light and entertaining without offending people or getting out of line."

Some of his classmates did not appreciate George's brand of humor, however. They thought he was too social and not studious enough. One classmate said if anyone had told George's fellow students when he attended Andover that he would one day run for president, there would have been gales of laughter.

By all accounts, it was at Andover that George developed his ability to relate to others and to be successful as a leader. Though he was never the student his father had been, his grades were acceptable. He left Andover with a diploma, a sense of self-confidence, and an easy manner with people. In spite of his early difficulties with his studies, by the time he graduated George had a new appreciation for education. This interest in education would one day become a major part of his political *platform*.

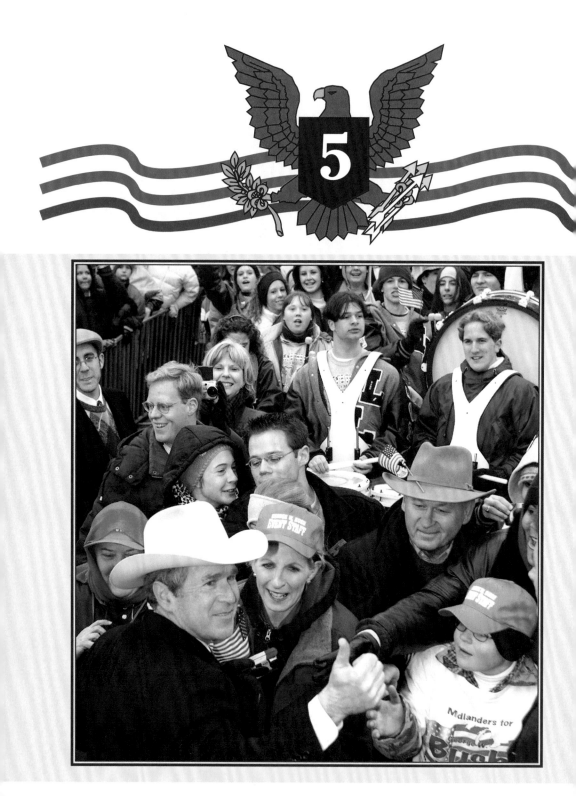

President-elect George W. Bush greets well-wishers as he prepares to depart Midland for Washington, D.C., and his inauguration, January 17, 2001.

From Texas to the White House

*I*n the summer of 1964, George returned to Texas. He traveled with his dad during George H. W. Bush's unsuccessful campaign for the U.S. Senate. In the fall George enrolled at Yale University in New Haven, Connecticut.

He graduated from Yale in 1968. In November of that year, he enlisted in the Texas Air National Guard and started F-102 pilot training at Moody Air Force Base in Georgia. He graduated as a second lieutenant in December 1969 and served in the Guard until 1973.

During his time in the National Guard, George worked for several political campaigns. He also spent a year in an inner-city program in Houston called Project PULL (Professional Unities Leadership League), working with inner-city boys. When asked why he got involved in Project PULL, he answered, "I was raised by a mother and father who taught the virtue of compassion. . . . I wanted to make a difference."

From 1973 to 1975 George attended Harvard Business School in Cambridge, Massachusetts. Harvard is considered by many to be the most prestigious business school in the world. After graduation, George returned to Midland, where

he started his own oil business. Once he became better known there, he decided to make his first run for political office, for the U.S. House of Representatives. While he was working on this campaign, he met Laura Welch, a native of Midland.

The friends who introduced them wondered whether George and Laura would be a good match. George has described their different personalities: "Laura is calm; I am energetic. She is restful; I am restless. She is patient; I am impatient. [But] we share the same values. We share a West Texas upbringing . . . and we both, very quickly, fell in love with each other." The couple married on November 5, 1977, just a few

George and Laura Bush on the campaign trail in West Texas and in a Bush for Congress poster (inset). In his first run for public office, George W. Bush failed to win a seat in the House of Representatives.

months after their first meeting.

Although George lost his political campaign, he continued to manage his oil company in Midland. In early 1981 Laura became pregnant with twins. Their daughters, Jenna and Barbara, were born on November 25 of that year.

It would be impossible to understand President George W. Bush without considering the depth of his personal faith. His spiritual side was obvious to many after the terrorist attacks. The *New York Times* reported that after September 11, "[Some] who are close to the president said there was a discernible spiritual dimension to his thinking."

During the mid-1980s, that spiritual dimension helped lead to what George has called "a turning point" in his life. Over the years, he had started drinking heavily. This began to concern people around him. "Gradually," he said, "drinking began to compete with my energy. I'd be a step slower getting up. My daily runs seemed harder after a few too many drinks the night before."

While vacationing at Kennebunkport in 1985, he was introduced to the Christian evangelist Billy Graham, a family friend. While talking with Graham, George felt that a seed of change was planted in his heart. "He led me to the path," George said, "and I began walking. And it was the beginning of a change in my life. . . . That weekend my faith took on new meaning." The following year, at a 40th birthday party, he decided that he would never drink again. He has kept to that decision ever since.

George and his family moved to Washington in 1988 to work on his father's presidential campaign. Poppy Bush won the election and became the 41st president of the United States. During this time in the capital, George W. Bush gained more political experience and made new contacts.

In 1989 George learned that the Texas Rangers, a major-league baseball team, was for sale. He joined with some wealthy people who agreed to put their money together and buy the team. He invested $600,000 and became a managing general partner of the Rangers. During his involvement with the team, a new stadium was built

President Bush is sometimes called "Dubya" because that's the way Texans pronounce his middle initial, "W."

The Bushes with their twin daughters, Jenna and Barbara, in Kennebunkport, Maine, 1991.

and the value of the Rangers soared. When George sold his share of the team in 1994, he received $15 million.

That same year, he ran for governor of Texas against Democrat Ann Richards, who was running for a second term. George won that election. During his first term, his popularity grew, and he was easily reelected to a second term in 1998. As governor he worked for new juvenile criminal laws, prison and education reforms, and tax cuts. He also pushed government support for faith-based programs.

During his second term, Governor Bush decided to compete as a Republican candidate for the presidency in the year 2000. He won the Republican Party's presidential nomination

When he was a managing partner of the Texas Rangers, George W. Bush got to know everyone working for the Rangers, including the hot dog vendors. He often sat in the stands rather than in the owners' boxes because he wanted to meet fans as well.

A lifelong baseball fan, George W. Bush jumped at the opportunity to join a group of investors who bought the major-league Texas Rangers team. Here he is seen with his father and Joe Morgan, an announcer and former baseball star.

in the summer of 2000. In the fall election, he would face the Democratic candidate, Al Gore, who had been vice president for the previous eight years.

The election of 2000 was a controversial one because it was so close. On election night, November 7, the outcome was uncertain. The focus of the election finally centered on Florida. Whoever received that state's votes in the *electoral college* would win the presidency. After weeks of debate and legal challenges over how the votes in Florida should be counted, Bush was declared the winner in that state. Although Al Gore had actually received about 500,000 more votes nationally than Bush, the Florida electoral votes gave Bush a narrow majority, 271 to 266. As a result, George W. Bush became the 43rd president of the United States.

History alone will determine the success of George Walker Bush's presidency. While he has many supporters, he also has had many critics. During the campaign and in his first year as president, he was often ridiculed because of his *malapropisms* and mocked for not being knowledgeable about world affairs. Some people said he ran for office on his father's reputation rather than his own.

However, even his critics have admitted he successfully mobilized the U.S. military and American allies for the so-called war on terrorism and won a decisive victory in that war's first battle, in Afghanistan. There America and her allies routed members of *al-Qaeda*, the terrorist group that sponsored the September 11 attacks, along with the Afghan government that harbored the terrorists, called the *Taliban*.

Yet that success alone will probably not be enough to guarantee George W. Bush's place in history. As one magazine reported, "increasingly he will be graded—both by America's voters and by the world outside—on the basis of longer-lasting achievements, on bills passed and wars concluded." But whatever the future for the 43rd president, his steadiness following September 11, 2001, will always be remembered by Americans who lived through the terrible events of that day.

> **George H. W. Bush and George W. Bush were the first father and son to become president since John Adams served as the second president (1797–1801) and John Quincy Adams as the sixth (1825–1829).**

CHRONOLOGY

1946 George Walker Bush born on July 6 in New Haven, Connecticut, to George Herbert Walker Bush and Barbara Pierce Bush.

1948 Moves with family to Odessa, Texas.

1950 Bush family settles in Midland.

1952 George begins first grade at Sam Houston Elementary School.

1958 Enters San Jacinto Junior High School for seventh grade.

1959 Bush family moves to Houston; George begins eighth grade at Kinkaid, a private school in Houston.

1961 Enters Phillips Academy, a private all-boys school in Andover, Massachusetts.

1964 Graduates from Phillips and begins studies at Yale University.

1968 Graduates from Yale; enlists in the Texas Air National Guard and becomes a pilot.

1973 Discharged from the Texas Air National Guard; enrolls at Harvard Business School.

1975 Graduates from Harvard Business School and forms an oil business in Midland, Texas.

1977 Launches unsuccessful run for a seat in the House of Representatives; meets Laura Welch and marries her on November 5.

1981 Twin daughters Jenna and Barbara born November 25.

1988 Father, George H.W. Bush, is elected president of the United States.

1989 Becomes part owner of the Texas Rangers baseball team and serves as a managing general partner.

1994 Sells his interest in the Texas Rangers; elected governor of Texas.

1998 Reelected governor of Texas by a wide margin.

2000 Wins the Republican Party's nomination for president in August; narrowly defeats Democrat Al Gore in an extremely close and controversial election.

2001 Sworn in as the 43rd president of the United States on January 20; on September 11, terrorists attack the United States by flying hijacked passenger airplanes into the World Trade Center and the Pentagon; United States and allies attack terrorists in Afghanistan.

Air Force One—the airplane that is used to transport the president of the United States.

al-Qaeda—a worldwide, anti-American and anti-Western terrorist organization that was founded by a wealthy Saudi named Osama bin Laden.

demerits—marks, usually resulting in lost privileges or punishment, that are given to a student who breaks the rules.

electoral college—a body composed of special voters (called electors), which meets after the general election to cast ballots for the president and vice president based on the results of the popular voting in the states. The candidate who wins the most votes in a state wins all of that state's electors, and the number of electors each state is allotted equals the number of U.S. senators and representatives from that state.

hemorrhage—a large discharge of blood from ruptured blood vessels, either internally or externally.

impromptu—made or done on the spur of the moment.

lacerate—to cut or tear with a jagged edge.

leukemia—an often fatal disease marked by an abnormal increase in the number of white blood cells.

malapropism—an unintentional misuse of words that sound similar, with a result that is often humorous or ridiculous.

nurture—to help someone (often a child) grow and develop.

outhouse—an outdoor toilet consisting of a small building that encloses a seat with a hole in it built over a pit.

Pentagon—a building outside Washington, D.C., that is the headquarters for the United States Department of Defense.

platform—publicly announced policies of a person seeking election.

sibling—a brother or sister.

synonym—a word that is similar in meaning to another word.

Taliban—an extremely conservative Islamic government that ruled Afghanistan between 1998 and 2001.

thesaurus—a reference book that contains words and their synonyms.

FURTHER READING

Bush, Barbara. *Barbara Bush: A Memoir.* New York: Charles Scribner and Sons, 1994.

Bush, George. *All the Best: My Life in Letters and Other Writings.* New York: Charles Scribner and Sons, 1999.

Bush, George W. *A Charge to Keep: My Journey to the White House.* New York: HarperCollins, 1999.

Degregorio, William A. *The Complete Book of U.S. Presidents.* Fort Lee, N.J.: Barricade Books, 2001.

Gormley, Beatrice: *President George W. Bush: Our Forty-third President.* New York: Aladdin Paperbacks, 2001.

Minutaglio, Bill. *First Son and the Bush Family Dynasty.* New York: Random House, 1999.

Mitchell, Elizabeth. *Revenge of the Bush Dynasty.* New York: Hyperion, 2000.

INTERNET RESOURCES

- http://www.historycentral.com/elections/georgewbush.html
  A brief biography of George W. Bush, written before the 2000 presidential election

- http://www.whitehouse.gov/kids/president/
  Facts about President Bush on a website geared especially toward children

- http://www.whitehouse.gov/president/
  The official White House website

INDEX

Bush, Barbara Pierce (mother), 13,
     14, 15, 20, 22–23, 26
Bush, Barbara (daughter), 37
Bush, Dorothy Walker (sister), 26
Bush, George Herbert Walker
     "Poppy" (father), 13, 14, 15, 18,
     19, 20, 23, 24, 25, 27, 29, 35, 38
Bush, George Walker
  adult accomplishments of, 9–11,
     35–41
  and baseball, 23, 24–25, 26, 30,
     38–39
  birth and childhood of, 14, 15,
     17–27
  and death of sister, 20–23, 30
  and father's political career, 27, 35,
     38
  high school years of, 29–33
  and September 11, 2001, terrorist
     attack, 9–11, 41
Bush, Jenna (daughter), 37
Bush, John Ellis "Jeb" (brother), 19, 20
Bush, Laura Welch (wife), 9, 36–37
Bush, Marvin (brother), 25
Bush, Neil Mallon (brother), 25
Bush, Pauline Robinson "Robin"
     (sister), 15, 18, 20, 21, 30
Bush, Prescott (grandfather), 32
Bush-Overbey Oil Development
     Company, 18

Cape Cod, 13
Capitol, 9

Florida, 9, 40–41

Gore, Al, 40
Gonzalez, José R., 32
Graham, Billy, 38

Harvard Business School, 35–36
Houston, Texas, 26, 27, 35

Kennebunkport, Maine, 23, 38
Kidde, John, 30
Kinkaid School, 26–27
Lyons, Tom, 30

Midland, Texas, 15, 17–18, 19, 20, 24,
     25, 26, 36
Moody Air Force Base, 35

New Haven, Connecticut, 13, 35

Odessa, Texas, 14, 15
Overbey, John, 18

Pearl Harbor, 13
Pennsylvania, 9
Pentagon, 9
Phillips Academy, 27, 29, 30–33
Pierce, Franklin, 13

Richards, Ann, 39
Roden, Randy, 18, 19

Sam Houston Elementary School, 19
San Jacinto Junior High School, 25

Texas Rangers baseball club, 38–39

Walker, Elsie, 21
Washington, D.C., 10, 38
White House, 9, 10
Wood, Michael M., 30
World Trade Center, 9
World War II, 13

Yale University, 13, 35

Zapata Company, 25
Zapata-Offshore Company, 25

PICTURE CREDITS

Contributors

ARTHUR M. SCHLESINGER JR. holds the Albert Schweitzer Chair in the Humanities at the Graduate Center of the City University of New York. He is the author of more than a dozen books, including *The Age of Jackson*; *The Vital Center*; *The Age of Roosevelt* (3 vols.); *A Thousand Days: John F. Kennedy in the White House*; *Robert Kennedy and His Times*; *The Cycles of American History*; and *The Imperial Presidency*. Professor Schlesinger served as Special Assistant to President Kennedy (1961–63). His numerous awards include the Pulitzer Prize for History; the Pulitzer Prize for Biography; two National Book Awards; the Bancroft Prize; and the American Academy of Arts and Letters Gold Medal for History.

BILL THOMPSON graduated from Boston University with a degree in education. After teaching history in public schools, Mr. Thompson earned a Master of Divinity from Colgate-Rochester and became a Presbyterian minister. He pastored in New York, New Jersey, and Florida. He and his wife, Dorcas, now live in Swarthmore, Pennsylvania. They have collaborated on several books, including *Geronimo* (Chelsea House, 2002) and *The Spanish Exploration of Florida* (Mason Crest, 2003).

DORCAS (BOARDMAN) THOMPSON graduated from Wheaton College in Illinois with a bachelor's degree in history. She taught history and social studies in Massachusetts and Pennsylvania. She has served as librarian in a private school and worked as an editor for an educational publisher in Massachusetts. The Thompsons have one daughter, Rebecca Mandia, who along with her husband, Albert, is an elementary-school teacher in Newtown, Pennsylvania, and one granddaughter, Rachel Elizabeth Mandia.